Naseem's Journey

Anjuli Farmay
Ilustrated by Joshua Wichterich

<u>Dedication</u>

To my husband, Soufiane, and our sweet children, Nabil, Ilyas and Zahra Sayhi.

Thanks for your unconditional love and encouragement.

Published in 2019 by Anjuli Farmay

For more information please contact farmayanjuli@gmail.com

Illustrated by Joshua Wichterich

ISBN-13: 978-1986119801

Whoosh! The airplane rumbled as it took off into the sky. It was Naseem's very first plane ride. He was on his way to visit the place in Morocco where his father grew up.

Naseem always wanted to visit Morocco. His daddy told him so many fun stories about living there. He was also excited to meet the family that he talked to each week from his computer.

"We're almost there," said Daddy, excitedly. Naseem looked out of the window. The view from the sky was amazing! He saw the ocean and mountains far below.

"You know, if you look hard enough, you might even see the desert," said Daddy. "Did you grow up in the desert?" asked Naseem. "No, I grew up in a village in the *Atlas Mountains*. It's far from the desert."

The plane finally landed. "Welcome to Morocco," the pilot said. Naseem's stomach was full of butterflies. He was ready for their journey to begin.

The airport was full of people visiting Morocco from all over the world. Naseem wondered if it was their first time, too.

They quickly started their drive up the mountains. Naseem had never been on a road so curvy. Around and around, twisting and turning they went. It felt like they were on a rollercoaster ride!

"Let's stop at the market and buy a box of sweets for the family," Daddy suggested. Naseem saw so many different types. He saw some with jam, some with chocolate and some with honey. They looked so crunchy and delicious.

"Welcome to *Telout*!" Daddy said. They were so high in the mountains that they felt like they could touch the clouds. It was amazing!

It wasn't long before they reached Daddy's house.
"I'll knock on the door!" said Naseem

Grandma answered the door. The rest of the family followed behind her. "Oh, we are so happy to finally meet you!" they said. Naseem was happy too. He had always dreamed of this day.

Grandma invited them into the living room. The smell of mint tea and freshly baked bread filled the air. Naseem saw so many treats on the table. There were cakes, cookies and pancakes. "Mmmmm!" he said.

"Would you like to play soccer with us?" asked Naseem's cousin. Soccer was his favorite sport. Naseem quickly agreed. He followed his cousins outside. Many other kids joined them.

They had so much fun playing soccer together. He really liked his new friends. They even taught him new words in Tashelheet and Arabic.

Naseem told his daddy all about his new friends. "Let's go for a walk now, Daddy, and see more of the village. I want to see everything."

"Do you see this house?" asked Daddy. "When I was a kid, people use to say a witch lived there." "Yikes!" shouted Naseem. That sounded spooky.

As they continued their walk, they passed apple trees and grape vines. " Here, climb on my shoulders and grab some apples," said Daddy. Naseem grabbed an apple and took a bite. He had never tasted fruit so juicy and sweet.

"Look! There's Aunt Fadma at the barn. Let's go see the animals," said Naseem. He loved animals. He saw sheep, chickens, a cow and even a donkey.

"Moo! Baa! Cock-a-doodle-doo!"
Naseem tried to copy all of the different sounds they made.
Aunt Fadma laughed as she watched him.

All of a sudden, he heard the call to prayer coming from the *mosque*. It was his favorite sound in the whole world. Everyone in the village stopped what they were doing to pray. "Let's join them," Naseem said. He loved going to the *mosque*.

On their way home, they passed by the neighbors. "*Assalam alaykum*." they said. Naseem liked the way they greeted each other with "Peace be upon you." "*Wa-Alaykum Salam*," he answered, which meant, "and unto you peace."

The neighbors invited them inside to share some *couscous*. It reminded him of tiny balls of pasta. "Yum! My favorite!" said Naseem, rubbing his belly. It was the most delicious *couscous* he had ever tasted.

Boom. Boom. Boom. The sound of a beating drum made Naseem step outside to see what was going on. "We are having a very special song and dance called *Ahwach*," Grandma explained.

Everyone was there, even Naseem's new friends. They started shaking their shoulders and stomping their feet to the beat of the drum. Naseem loved dancing. "Look at me Daddy; I'm shaking my shoulders really fast." He giggled.

"I'm having a lot of fun here said Naseem, as they walked home.
"I am going to miss it here when we go back to America."

" Me too ," said Daddy. "Being far away from family, friends, and the place where you grew up is hard sometimes.

"I have an idea. We can call both places home!"
Naseem exclaimed. Daddy smiled. "I like that idea,
Naseem. It's wonderful to have two beautiful places
to call home."

Glossary

Ahwach: a style of collective performance that is popular in Southern Morocco.

Assalamu Alaykum/Walaykum Salam: a greeting that means, "peace be upon you," commonly used by people of the Islamic faith.

Atlas Mountains : a mountain range in northern Africa ranging from Morocco to Tunisia.

Couscous: a North African dish of steamed semolina.

Mosque: a place of worship for people of the Islamic faith.

Tashelheet: an Amazigh/Berber indigenous language spoken in Morocco.

Telouet: a village in the Atlas Mountains of Morocco.

Inspired by a True Story

Telouet is a Berber village located in the High Atlas region of Morocco. The village is famous for the Telouet Kasbah and traditional Berber dance. My story was inspired by my children's first experience visiting their father's family in Telouet. We shared many beautiful memories there. I hope this story will help them remember their special journey.

Naseem's Favorite Moroccan Pancakes

Beghrir is a spongy, honeycomb pancake popular in the Maghreb region of Africa. It's best served with butter and honey.

Ingredients
- 1 1/2 cups fine semolina or durum flour
- 3/4 cup all-purpose flour
- 1 teaspoon salt
- 1 teaspoon sugar
- 2 teaspoon baking powder
- 1 tablespoon yeast
- 3 cups plus 2 tablespoons lukewarm water

Directions
1. Mix the semolina, flour, salt, sugar and baking powder in a mixing bowl. In a blender, measure lukewarm water to just over the 3-cup line. Add the yeast and process on low speed to blend. Gradually add the dry ingredients.
2. Increase the processing speed and blend for a full minute, or until very smooth and creamy. The batter should be rather thin, about the same consistency as crepe batter or cooking cream.
3. Pour the batter into a bowl. Cover with plastic wrap and leave to rest for 10 minutes or a bit longer, until the top of the batter is light and a bit foamy.

4. Heat a small non-stick skillet over medium heat. Stir the batter, and use a ladle to pour batter into the hot skillet. Pour carefully and slowly into the center and the batter will spread evenly into a circle. (Do not swirl the pan as you would for a crepe; the batter should spread itself.) Make the beghrir as large as you like.

5. Bubbles should appear on the surface of the beghrir as it cooks. Don't flip the beghrir. It only gets cooked on one side.

6. Cook for about two minutes, or until the beghrir doesn't appear wet anywhere on the surface. It should feel spongy, but not sticky or gummy when you touch it lightly with your finger.

7. Transfer the beghrir to cool in a single layer on a clean kitchen towel. Once they are cool, they can be stacked without sticking.

8. Repeat with the remaining batter. Serve plain with toppings on the side, or dip the pancakes in hot syrup.

Recipe by Christine Benlafquih. For more Moroccan recipes, see tasteofmaroc.com.

About the Author

Anjuli earned a degree in International Studies from Meredith College. Her multicultural upbringing in the small town of Loris , South Carolina influenced her love for languages and world cultures. Her book, "Naseem's Journey" was inspired by her children's first experience visiting their father's village in Morocco. She currently resides in North Carolina, United States with her husband and three kids. This is Anjuli's first children's book.

prayersandcrayons.blog

Made in the USA
Middletown, DE
04 December 2023

44664670R00022